My River

Cleaning up the LaHave River

My River

Cleaning up the LaHave River

STELLA BOWLES
WITH ANNE LAUREL CARTER

Formac Publishing Company Limited
Halifax

Formac Publishing Company Limited recognizes the support of the Province of Nova
Scotia through the Department of Communities, Culture and Heritage. We are pleased to
work in partnership with the Province of Nova Scotia to develop and promote our cultural
resources for all Nova Scotians. We acknowledge the support of the Canada Council for
the Arts, which last year invested $153 million to bring the arts to Canadians throughout
the country. This project has been made possible in part by the Government of Canada.

The author acknowledges funding support from the Ontario Arts Council (OAC), an
agency of the Government of Ontario.

Cover design: Tyler Cleroux
Cover image: Andrea Conrad

Photo Credits: All photos were taken by Andrea Conrad except for the following:
Berrigan, Jane: p. 85; Bowles, Lender: p. 89; Coastal Action: p. 45; LighthouseNOW: p. 56

Map Credit: The map on p. 32 is included courtesy of Coastal Action.

Cataloguing in Publication information is available from Library and Archives Canada.

Published by:
Formac Publishing
Company Limited
5502 Atlantic Street
Halifax, NS, Canada
B3H 1G4
www.formac.ca

Distributed in Canada by:
Formac Lorimer Books
5502 Atlantic Street
Halifax, NS, Canada
B3H 1G4

Distributed in the US by:
Lerner Publisher Services
1251 Washington Ave. N.
Minneapolis, MN, USA
55401
www.lernerbooks.com

Printed and bound in Canada.
Manufactured by Friesens Corporation in Altona, Manitoba,
Canada in July 2018.
Job # 245951

Contents

Foreword

I grew up on the Don River in Toronto. It was ugly. It stank. When the Queen's sister, Princess Margaret, came to visit in 1958 the adults knew they had to do something. They dumped perfume in it for an hour. Suds floated on the surface. So did dead fish. My older sister wondered, what's killing the fish? A teacher let her study minnows from the river in a school aquarium — she didn't find the pollution culprit but she got hooked by science. Her curiosity led her to a Ph.D. in botany and a life-long commitment to protect nature.

Stella Bowles reminds me of my sister. Stella has a scientist's curiosity. She lives in Nova Scotia on a polluted river, the LaHave, and studied it for Grade 6 and 7 science fair projects.

In 2003, I bought an old house on the LaHave. I saw people swim in the river and hoped I could one day. In 2015, I finally built a wharf and dock and went for my first swim. A friend drove over and yelled, "Quick! Get out, Anne! Haven't you seen the sign Stella Bowles made?"

I drove up the river to see Stella's sign. I never went swimming again.

Stella shared the results of her science project in many creative ways. She succeeded in shaming three levels of government — municipal, provincial and federal — plus an anonymous donor into funding a $15.7 million cleanup.

Stella had the one thing my sister lacked to succeed. It's what every activist needs to become a perfect storm of change. This story will tell you why and how she did it.

— Anne Laurel Carter

Thank you, Anne Laurel Carter, for caring about our river and coming to me and suggesting the book idea. I am so thankful you have put my story in a book. I really hope it inspires more kids to fight for causes they are passionate about.

— Stella Bowles

Chapter 1
Our River's Got a Dirty Secret

My name is Stella Bowles and I live with my parents, my brother, William and our dog, Zappa, on the LaHave River in Nova Scotia. I'm thirteen years old and in Grade 8.

I live outside a small town called Bridgewater. My house overlooks the river. There's a road between our front yard and our wharf where we have a small motorboat and sailboat. My mom's family has lived on this property since 1780 when the river was the *only* way to get anywhere and everyone fished for a living or for their supper.

I've always wanted to swim off our wharf. It bugs me that I can't. On warm sunny days in summer, I watch other kids dive and splash around and beg my parents, "Please, can I go in?"

Mom always said, "No. That's why we have an above-ground pool. You can swim there."

I didn't find out *why* until before Grade 6 started.

You won't believe the reason. I didn't.

I only found out because part of our front yard turned into a swamp. It stank, and not like flowers. Mom said there was a problem with our septic system and made phone calls.

An engineer came to see what the problem was.

My brother, William, my dad, Lennie, me, and my mom, Andrea. That's our dalmatian, Zappa, in the front.

Did you know?

The LaHave River is 97-km long and fresh water where it begins in the Annapolis Valley. It flows past the town of Bridgewater and mixes with salt water before joining the Atlantic Ocean.

"You have a very old septic system," he said. "The bed has collapsed. You have three months to fix it."

"Excuse me?" Mom said, and pointed around the river. "All those houses have straight pipes. Do they have three months to fix their problem?"

He laughed. "I'm required by law to say that." He winked as if it was a big joke. "Don't worry about it. No one checks."

As far as he was concerned, the problem was over and he drove away. It wasn't over for my mom. She cares a lot about our home. She banged around the kitchen, making a salad to accompany Dad's amazing dinner. We'd gone jigging for squid that morning and he'd spent hours preparing calamari the way William and I liked it.

We sat around the table and devoured the calamari.

"I can't believe it. No one checks our septic systems?" Mom said, tossing the salad. "We have laws against it for a reason. It's not right to keep ignoring it."

"What's illegal?" I asked, confused. "What's the *it* being ignored?"

"People still use straight pipes."

"What's a straight pipe?"

"Pipes that let you flush what's in your toilet straight into a lake or ocean or river."

Did you know?

Two hundred and fifty years ago my ancestors got land from an Acadian family and built a house close to their fishing wharf. Remember pioneers? They all used an outhouse for the bathroom. Pretty cold in winter. When my grandfather built a new house, he installed indoor plumbing AND a septic system in the front yard to let the ground clean the dirty water. He didn't want to use a straight pipe like many of his neighbours.

"What's in your toilet —" I gagged. "Poop? Our neighbours are pooping in the LaHave?"

I looked out the kitchen window, past the front yard, the road and our wharf to the water. Now I was upset. I take after my mom that way. "How many straight pipes?" I asked.

"No one knows," Mom said.

"Is that why you never let us swim in the river?"

"Yes."

William spat out his calamari. "You mean it's like a big toilet? I'm not eating fish from a toilet. And you let me take sailing lessons this summer? You saw me turtle. Why did you sign me up?"

Mom turned pale. "I'm sorry."

Dad interrupted. "Hold on. Mom didn't do anything wrong. You're getting worked up over nothing. It's not a big toilet. No one gets sick from the river. It's perfectly safe to swim in."

"With poop in it? It's totally disgusting," I said.

"Totally gross," William said.

Mom nodded. "When I was growing up, the Department of Health tested it regularly and put up signs saying, 'No Swimming. Fecal Contamination'. Then the signs suddenly stopped."

"Because the river's cleaner," Dad said.

"Because they didn't want to pay for testing anymore."

I stared at the LaHave again. In my mind, I renamed it Poo River. "Fish live in the river," I said. "Is it healthy for fish, Dad?"

"Tides flush the river clean every day." His calm face said this wasn't a big problem.

"What about the shallows? What if poop settles there?" I stared at William, remembering a month earlier when I ferried him in our aluminum boat to the learn-to-sail camp at the little yacht club across the LaHave. I saw boats turtle, dumping kids in the water. One time William's boat flipped close to shore. The mast stuck in the bottom. When they got it upright the top of the sail was covered in what looked like poop. Mom was so grossed out she took a picture of it.

I had lots of questions. I was worried because my dad and William loved to sail on the river. They waded into the river at our wharf and sometimes fell in, too.

I needed to find out if Poo River could make them sick.

William and other kids taking the boats out of the water at the LaHave River Yacht Club.

Chapter 2
Can Poop in Water Make You Sick?

I googled my question: Can swimming in poopy water make you sick?

I didn't like the answer.

In September, our neighbours had a backyard wedding. It was a beautiful warm Saturday. I was horrified when I heard splashing.

They were swimming.

I wanted to run out and tell them, "Get out! There's poop in the water."

Dad stopped me. "Don't bother those people. They're having a good time."

"What if they get sick? What if you and William get sick? You're always wading in to fix the anchor or the pulley system or something."

"Do I look sick?" Dad made a goofy face.

I laughed because he's funny. But it didn't stop me from asking my next question.

"Do people know it's illegal?"

"Probably," Dad said.

"Why don't they get taken to court?"

"Like Judge Judy? Straight pipes have been around a long time. They're all over Canada. Installing a septic system is expensive and some people can't afford it."

"Can I find out exactly how much poop is in the water?"

Dad turned thoughtful. If William and I are really interested in something, he listens and tries to help us. So does my mom.

"Probably. The Department of Health or Environment must know."

Mom said, "Or organizations who protect the environment. I'll phone around tomorrow."

Mom made a lot of phone calls. At supper, she told us that the Bluenose Coastal Action Foundation — now called Coastal Action — in

Yep! This is a straight pipe. Totally gross! You can even see the wet toilet paper. YUCK!

Lunenburg was considered the best source of information and was a charitable organization committed to studying and protecting the ecosystem of the South Shore of Nova Scotia. A retired doctor, Dr. Maxwell, was one of their go-to experts. He lived on the LaHave and had been testing the fecal contamination for over two years. His results were reported to committees and the government.

"Dr. Maxwell is also part of a local community Straight Pipe Committee," Mom said. "They're concerned citizens who lobby the government. The results of the tests are bad."

"Is the government doing anything?" I asked.

"No."

"Why not? All they have to do is google what I did. Dirty water isn't safe. Dad fell in last week. I want to do something." I had an idea. "If the government won't put up a sign, can we?"

So that's what we did.

We designed a big, bold sign to tell people what the government wasn't. I talked to our neighbours first. They didn't mind. In fact, they said, "It's about time. Go for it!"

Even though my dad thought we were heading for disappointment, he helped us. He built a frame and we put it up right beside the road and the river. On our property.

Everyone driving by saw it. Everyone started talking about it. Some people didn't believe it. Some did.

Some people never went swimming again.

I put up this sign so everyone driving by could read it and be warned.

Chapter 3
Science is a Blast

Science is often boring at school. All we do is read textbooks and study for tests. No one likes it.

But at home? My dad makes science fun.

We used to make rockets and shoot them off in our backyard. That was a blast (one of my dad's jokes). Dad used to work at the Discovery Centre in Halifax because he loved science. He often took us there when we drove into the city. I grew up believing science was like the name of the place: *discovery*.

In Grade 5 we had to do a project for the science fair competition. I designed one to let other kids discover something cool about bubbles. Everyone thinks bubbles are fragile and easy to pop, right? But if you dip a stick into bubble solution and pull up a bubble sheet, you can immerse your other hand in the solution, reach through the bubble sheet and . . . the bubble wall won't break.

Try it yourself. A bubble will wrap around anything wet and not pop.

The important part of my science project was letting kids *discover* bubble behaviour for themselves. This meant bringing a bucket of bubble solution into the gym where our projects were on display.

At school, however, the teacher scowled at me and my bucket. "You can't bring that in here. If it spills, it will harm the floor. Your poster is good enough."

There was no arguing with that teacher. All day kids came into the gym and asked about my project. All I could do was repeat what it said on my poster. I was a talking textbook.

The bubble machine I built with my dad. I never got to present it at school.

When I got home, I threw my backpack on the floor. Not something I'd normally do.

My mom asked what was wrong.

I cried. All day I'd followed a rule that made no sense and wrecked my project. Something inside me burst like a bubble. Mom listened as I talked about why I liked science and my frustrations at school. The rules were too strict. I didn't fit in. The girls bullied me.

By Grade 6, I'd changed schools. Mom warned me that changing schools doesn't always solve a kid's problems, but mostly it did for me. I already had friends there. I fit in and was happier. The rules made sense.

What about science? I had great expectations especially when we went to a lab for science class. We partnered off and began to collect glass beakers for our first experiment. Suddenly there was a crash. Two kids accidentally dropped a beaker and then . . . a second crash.

The teacher lost it. "That's enough! No more! Get out your textbooks."

It was disappointing. But it wasn't a huge loss for me. I could do science at home.

In September after Grade 6 started, Mom found out about a meeting of the LaHave River Straight Pipe Committee. Dr. Maxwell would be there and I decided to attend, so we went.

I listened to the adults talk about how offensive they found straight pipes. They were frustrated. As a group, they'd worked hard at bringing the issue to the government's attention for over two years. Before the last election, every candidate promised they'd enforce the law as soon as they were in power. After the election? "Sorry. Too busy." Not only did they stop listening, at the last meeting with the MLA (Member of the Legislative Assembly) he told them not to come back.

Adults didn't make sense to me. Poop in the river was disgusting. End of story.

Would they listen to a kid? They might if I shamed them. I needed a new science project for the science fair in March and adults had dumped one in my front yard.

"How do I test water for contamination, Dad?"

Dad helped me do research on the internet. Testing turned out to be expensive. I'd need to submit each sample to an accredited lab to be tested and each test cost thirty dollars.

Even though Dad helped me do the research, he was convinced I wouldn't get any results. "You're heading for disappointment with this project."

"Straight pipes are illegal. Adults will be embarrassed that a kid is talking about it," I responded.

Dad was also looking for a job and we were living on Mom's salary. "It's not exactly in our budget right now."

"I'll make lots of jam and sell it."

Mom interrupted. "Let's phone Dr. Maxwell. He tested the water for two years. Maybe he'll have some advice."

I overheard her phone call to Dr. Maxwell and rolled my eyes as she described me to him. "Stella's shy. She gets no support for her interest in science at school. She wants to test the contamination of the LaHave River for a science fair project."

She didn't mention my dad's scepticism. Dr. Maxwell was busy but agreed to find time to talk to me in October.

I started making jam.

I can make a lot of jam fast if I know that I can sell it.

Chapter 4
Every Activist Needs a Dr. Maxwell

My dad was leaving to rehearse with his rock band when Dr. Maxwell arrived in October.

Dad opened the back door and with a straight face he said, "What's up, Doc?"

Dr. Maxwell hesitated before he stepped inside, not quite sure how to read my dad.

"I've always wanted to say that to a real doctor." Dad grinned at me, pleased with his joke, and I laughed. He was a big tease and just trying to be funny.

Mom welcomed Dr. Maxwell and we sat at the kitchen table.

Dr. Maxwell stared at my mom and then me. I knew what he saw: an eleven-year-old with chubby cheeks. I was glad he didn't look away or through me like I didn't count.

He still seemed hesitant and glanced at our car's headlights turning from our driveway onto the road. Did he want to leave, too?

"Let's get to the point of my visit," he said. "I've devoted my life to making people and the world healthy. I've been an activist since I was old enough to march."

Dr. Maxwell pointed at the river. "Fecal contamination in a waterway is unhealthy and preventable. What's your interest in the LaHave?"

He was staring at me, not my mom, curious to hear my reasons. He was very serious but I respected him as a doctor, as a trained scientist and as an expert testing the river. Besides, I'd only sold five jars of jam.

"Straight pipes are disgusting," I said.

"I wish I could swim in the river. My dad and brother sail on it. I want to test how safe the river is and display the results for my science project. Maybe if a kid says, 'straight pipes are disgusting,' adults will be shamed into ending them."

He cracked a smile. He liked my answer.

"Do you know what enterococci are?"

I shook my head.

"If you do this project, that's what you'll test for," he said. "I've tested the levels of enterococci in the LaHave for over two years. Salt water doesn't kill this organism. The results are always bad and can vary depending on location, season, weather and the tides. There are two numbers to watch for."

Yep, another straight pipe putting toxins in our river.

Did you know?

Enterococci are bacteria found in the intestines of warm-blooded animals and their fecal waste. In other words: in their poop. Scientists test the enterococci levels of water to measure fecal contamination.

My parents had our old septic system replaced right away when the problem was discovered.

He wrote them down in a chart I memorized.

"Do you know what happens to people who go in contaminated water?"

I told him what I learned after I googled my question about poop in water.

He nodded. "Poop in water was the big issue that modernized public health. About a hundred and fifty years ago, an English doctor proved that an outbreak of cholera in part of London was caused by human sewage getting into their source of drinking water. In the last century, science has shown us a much safer, smarter place to put human waste. Do you know where?"

I guessed. "In the ground?"

"Yes. That's why rural homes like yours and mine need a septic system in the yard."

"Ours is in our front yard and stopped working. It didn't smell safe. It's costing a lot of money to dig up our yard and put the new system in."

24

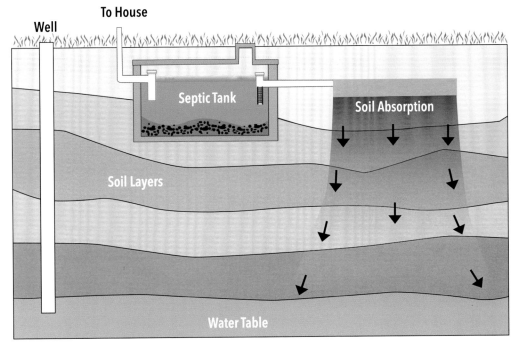

Diagram of a septic system

"If you lived in Bridgewater you wouldn't have this problem. Towns can build a big sewage treatment plant. Here's a sketch of how a basic septic system works."

He pointed to his sketch as he spoke. "Heavy material in the tank is called sludge. It sinks to the bottom. The effluent is lighter liquid. It flows out to the drain field where organisms in the ground eat and destroy the harmful bacteria, turning it into good fertilizer. Sludge back in the tank builds up over time and has to get pumped out and taken to sewage treatment plants or a special dump where it's turned into fertilizer."

"My brother got dumped in the LaHave this summer when his sailboat turtled. It happened a lot. One time, when they got the sail back up, it was covered in muck and it looked a lot like poop." I showed him a photo. "It's part of the reason I want to do my project on the contamination in the river."

They kept turtling the boat (flipping it over), so they got a tow to shore. Notice the gross stuff on the sail where it stuck in the sludge at the bottom of the river. YUCK!

"Your mom told me about your last school science project. Wasn't it a bad experience?"

I shrugged. "I still like science. And who knows? I might win the science fair."

He laughed. "Competitive, are we?"

"She plays hockey," my mom said. "She plays left wing; she's a team player, great at assists."

"Sports and science have something in common. Hard work. You need a winning hypothesis. Do you have one?"

"The LaHave River is safe to swim in," I said.

"For valid results, you'll need a control. If you're testing LaHave River water, what will your control be?"

I guessed. "Tap water."

"Ah, but what if there's a bit of enterococci bacteria in the tap water?"

"There isn't any . . . is there?" Suddenly I remembered camping. "I'll boil it first."

"Right."

I was impatient to ask him *my* questions. "About my project, I found out it costs thirty dollars to send each sample of water to a lab for testing. I've been making and selling strawberry jam, but I'm not going to make enough to fund a science project. How can I get the cost down?"

He turned quiet and seemed to make a decision. "You can test your water samples at home. I'll make you a testing kit from my extra supplies. I have an extra incubator I'll lend you. Next time I come over, I'll bring everything and teach you the procedure."

"Really?" I couldn't believe it. I stared at my mom. She seemed amazed, too.

"Do you think I could get people interested in cleaning up the river?"

"It's a long shot. They have to complain to the government. I didn't get anywhere, so you'll be the one holding the torch. But," he smiled, "if you don't succeed, you'll learn how to do science along the way. I'll enjoy teaching you."

There was only one thing to say. "Thank you, Dr. Maxwell. Would you like a jar of jam?"

Chapter 5
Getting Ready

In the first week of November, Dr. Maxwell came over with the equipment.

Dad watched him carry everything from his car to the house and opened the door for him.

"Hey, what's up, Doc?"

Dr. Maxwell didn't respond. Dad tried again. "And you brought your own oven. What are we making? Carrot cake?"

Dr. Maxwell said with a straight face, "It's an incubator for Stella's science project."

Dad wasn't done teasing. He took and held Dr. Maxwell's long pole like a sword. "You could patent this. Call it the Maxwell Pole. Great for catching things you don't want to touch."

Dr. Maxwell ignored Dad and turned to me. "You'll be growing fecal colonies in this incubator. Where do you want it?"

"Sounds gross. Not around food and not in my room. It's too cold outside . . ."

"The basement," Mom said firmly.

The basement was creepy. I never went down there.

"I'll take it down," Dad offered. "It's not exactly Stella's favourite place."

Dr. Maxwell put a box on the kitchen table. It felt like Christmas. He opened it and started taking the equipment out, naming each object as he explained its function in the testing procedure.

By the time he finished, I'd forgotten the first step.

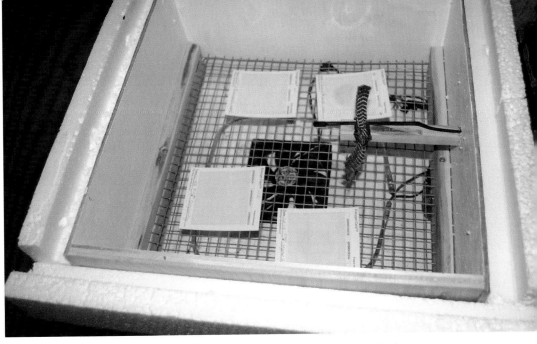

I grow poop bacteria in this incubator, in my creepy basement. Lol

"Could you repeat that? Slowly?"

"Sorry. I guess it's like following a new recipe with strange ingredients." He put everything back in the box. "You'll only learn by doing. Your turn."

I took everything out as he named and explained what to do with each piece of equipment again. I practiced a few times. It didn't take long to understand the procedure.

Dr. Maxwell was a great teacher. After I was able to demonstrate and describe the testing method, he stressed how careful a scientist had to be to make sure the results were valid.

"Nothing can contaminate the river water or the control if you want people to believe your results. That's the scientific method. I'll help you sterilize the testing bottles before you go into the river to get the samples. When you come home with the samples, I'll also be here to supervise and sterilize tap water

Equipment:

1. Filter funnel
2. Testing cards
3. Filters
4. Syringe
5. Plastic bottles
6. Long tweezers
7. Vacuum pump

Dr. Maxwell showed me how to do the science, step by step.

to be the control. You'll sterilize the filter funnel and tweezers in rubbing alcohol each time before you use them."

Suddenly it hit me: my science project wasn't just an idea. It was going to happen.

Excited, I turned to Mom. "Can we go out tomorrow?"

She reached for her iPad to check her work schedule but Dr. Maxwell held up his hand.

"Before we pick a date, you need to choose four sites. You

My method:

1. Test monthly at chosen sites.
2. Sterilize sample bottles in pressure cooker 20 minutes at 5 lb.
3. Label site and date and secure bottle onto 2-metre pole.
4. Remove cap — avoid contamination.
5. Wade in, reach out pole, submerge bottle 30 cm under surface.
6. Carefully secure cap onto sample bottle.
7. Use rubbing alcohol to sterilize all surfaces of testing equipment.
8. Pour 100 ml of sample through filter funnel with a membrane filter.
9. Use vacuum pump to suck water through funnel faster.
10. Place filter on a labelled nutrient medium card.
11. Incubate 36 hours at 36 degrees Celsius (body temperature).
12. Remove cards, count and record blue dots of enterococci colony.

should also choose if you want to test at high tide or low. These are variables and need to be consistent each time you test."

I picked four locations where I'd seen people swimming. "At the LaHave River Yacht Club on the other side of the river because of William. And Dayspring because it has a public boat launch. A lot of people go in there."

"What about Shipyards Landing in Bridgewater?" Mom suggested. "People go in the water there, too."

I nodded and named the fourth site, the one most important to me.

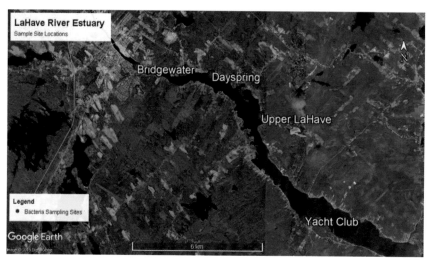

Map of testing locations

"Outside our house at our wharf in Upper LaHave. I'll test at low tide when it's easier to wade in."

They compared calendars while I checked a tide chart on the internet. The first day they were free from four to six in the evening at low tide was November 13.

One week. In a week, I'd conduct my first test. It was hard to wait.

Chapter 6
A Virtual Sign

I told a good friend about my project but otherwise I didn't talk about it at school.

The sign, however, was causing people to talk up a storm. People were discussing straight pipes and phoning the Municipality. Almost every night at the supper table my parents shared something they'd heard during the day from a neighbour or friend. People weren't happy because my sign was a daily reminder of a disgusting situation that needed fixing. People were phoning Coastal Action, the newspaper, two MLAs and the town council.

Another straight pipe! Can you imagine there are over 600 of these in my river. Actually, they are all over Nova Scotia. Have you ever seen one?

A friend's mother was involved in politics. She was getting phone calls. Their family was discussing my sign at their supper table. I realized signs were an effective way to share a message. We needed other ways to spread the word.

The next day, as soon as Mom got home from work, I cornered her. "You know how you help teachers with technology and social media? I need your help. I want to use social media to spread my message about straight pipes. I want you to create a Facebook page for my project."

Mom frowned. "I don't think that's a good idea."

"More people should know what's in the river," I said. "That's why we put the sign up."

"A Facebook page is a cyber sign. Kids don't use Facebook. Adults do and adults are voters. Facebook can reach more of them, not just the ones who drive past our house. More adults will complain about straight pipes if they know about the issue."

"You haven't even done your first test yet. Let's talk about this after you get your first results."

I was impatient to get the word out. I bugged Mom the next day. And the next.

Mom agreed with my goal but not social media. "I'm not putting your face out there. You're only eleven. The online world is scary and unpredictable. This is a topic that could become controversial. What if people challenge your results? What if people say hurtful things?"

"No one's said anything hurtful yet. And if there are people who don't like it, a Facebook page is a good way to find out. People should be free to leave their comments. All I want is for them to share it and spread the word."

"Let me go talk to your father."

Mom went upstairs for over an hour. She came back just as unhappy and still frowning.

"All right. We'll compromise. I'll make you a page, but I'm in complete control of it. If you want to post anything, we do it together. If people leave comments, I'll monitor them for anything inappropriate. At any point, I can shut down the page. Agreed?"

"Thanks, Mom."

She opened her laptop. "What do you want to call it?"

"The LaHave River: Stella's Science Project."

Here's my first post:

Hi, my name is Stella. I live along the LaHave River and I am very sad that I can't swim in my river. For years now, people have been flushing their toilets directly into the water through straight pipes. Straight pipes are illegal, but no one is telling people to stop. Pooping in our river is so gross and wrong. I decided to start a project on testing the river after my mom explained to me how high the fecal levels really are. Most people thought the river was getting healthier, but that just isn't true. Our river is very sick.

I am going to post my testing results here for the public to see. Maybe if more people know how much poop is in our river someone will fix it.

Chapter 7
Wading In

Collecting samples with **Dr.** Maxwell and the Maxwell **Pole**.

At my school, every student has to have an iPad.

I sat beside my friend and for the next two days one of us put our iPad under our desk to check my Facebook page. It was cool. My post reached 4,340 people and was shared fifty times. All the comments that were left supported my message. Most people were angry the government hadn't done anything

When doing the science, I have to be very careful and make sure the measurements are correct.

more than call straight pipes "illegal" in the Environment Act. Calling pollution illegal wasn't enough. It had to be enforced by government agencies in order to stop it.

Dr. Maxwell met us after school on November 13. We tested the river at our home wharf first. Mom drove me to the other three sites with the sterilized and labelled testing bottles. I wore my rubber boots and each time I waded out as far as I could with the Maxwell Pole and scooped up a sample of river water.

Wading back to shore at one of the locations, I noticed a metal hole marking the end of a straight pipe above the water. Below it in the shallows I saw things people had flushed down their toilets, things that hadn't been washed away in a tide or sunk to the bottom.

Sterilized tweezers make sure my testing cards do not get contaminated.

Gross things. Clumps of toilet paper. A tampon. A condom. A needle.

I brought the samples of river water back to our house. Dr. Maxwell met us there. He took one look at my face and said, "What's wrong?"

I told him about the nasty things I'd seen.

"When people flush the toilet they think, 'It's gone. It's not my problem now.' But as you saw, it's not gone. Everything flushed down a straight pipe becomes everyone's problem. Shall we get started?"

Dr. Maxwell supervised as I went through the procedure carefully and prepared the testing cards which were similar in size to the ones in a deck of playing cards.

Mom knew how I felt about the basement. We took the cards downstairs together to put in the incubator.

I thanked Dr. Maxwell and he said, "Phone me Sunday afternoon. If there are any problems, I'll come over."

What problems? We'd followed the procedure carefully. In thirty-six hours, I'd take the testing cards out, count the blue dots and have my first results.

A day and a half was a long time to wait. Thankfully it was the weekend. I had two hockey games. I'd focus on blue lines, not blue dots, and keep the puck away from our net.

Chapter 8
Poop Goes Viral

On Sunday morning, November 15, I was so excited I went down to the basement with my mom to take the testing cards out of the incubator myself.

I felt a wave of dismay as I stared at the five cards. One of them — the control — was supposed to be clear. There was a cluster of blue dots on all five cards.

We'd been so careful.

The test hadn't worked. A lump of disappointment grew in my throat.

"Let's take them upstairs," Mom said, trying to cheer me up. "Dr. Maxwell might be able to figure out what went wrong."

I called Dr. Maxwell and told him the bad news.

He laughed.

"Welcome to science. Every good scientist has failures. That's the fun part. Our challenge is to figure out where the contamination came from and what to do differently next time. I have a bit of work to finish here, then I'll come over and we'll solve the problem."

By the time he arrived, he'd figured out the answer. "The filters I gave you were from a sewage treatment facility. They weren't the right ones for this test. I just ordered the right ones from a lab. They come sterilized in a package and should arrive in ten days. You'll have to retest."

Mom interrupted, a little uncomfortable. "How much will they cost?"

"Leave that with me for a bit. The LaHave River Credit

Every month I went out and tested my four sites. It was easy on beautiful days like this. Winter was a different experience.

Union in Bridgewater sponsors local initiatives. They'll like Stella's project. After all, it's about the LaHave River."

He turned to me with a serious expression. "You have to anticipate all the possible criticisms people might make. Imagine your next test results appear valid, that the control is blank and the sites show contamination. Remember, you're testing at home. People need scientific proof that the results of your home testing are reliable."

I remembered our first conversation about the testing I couldn't afford. "They'd believe the government lab, right?" Dr. Maxwell nodded and I thought out loud. "I'll send a sample of river water to the lab and also test it at home, then compare the results."

I turned to Mom. "Christmas is coming. I can earn thirty dollars if I sell the rest of my jam to Nanny and her friends."

Dr. Maxwell laughed and interrupted. "Sell jam if you want, but Coastal Action already has a LaHave River water testing program in place with funding to send samples to the accredited government lab. It's the gold standard. I'm sure Coastal Action will share water samples so you can parallel test with your cards and validate your methodology."

They looked at their calendars while I checked the tide chart. We set my next test date for November 27.

Under the bright light over the kitchen counter I counted and recorded the blue dots on each test card so that I'd have a record for future reference. Here's what I found:

- LaHave River Yacht Club: 147 enterococci/100 ml
- My house, Upper LaHave: 320/100 ml
- Dayspring public wharf: 1,010/100 ml
- Shipyards Landing, Bridgewater: 3,020/100 ml

The results were good for my project, but horrible for the river. A reading above 70 per 100 ml meant the water was not safe to swim in.

"I need to post something on my Facebook page," I said. "I hope people haven't lost interest."

"It's like the next episode in a series," Mom said. "You have some followers. You're bound to get a few likes."

Here's what I posted:

> Science isn't always easy! The testing did not turn out as planned. The control sample showed some concerns, so I can't use the data and claim it is right. I am waiting for new supplies and then will redo my testing. Stay tuned!

That afternoon, a CBC reporter called, asking if I'd do a live interview on radio. Of course I said yes!

When the time came, the interviewer was friendly and put me at ease. "Just tell people what the issue is, about your sign and Facebook page and why you're doing this."

After the first question, I relaxed and found it easy to talk about the river. CBC also published an article about the project on the CBC Nova Scotia website with a photo of me holding the Maxwell Pole.

My Facebook page results were the biggest shock. Within days the post reached over 50,000 people. After ten days, my post had over 1,200 likes.

My poop river project had gone viral.

Chapter 9
Ducks Don't Use Toilet Paper

This is me getting a sample in Bridgewater. The weather was a bit colder now!

On November 27, the new filters arrived just in time for Dr. Maxwell to bring them over after school. He sterilized the testing bottles in a pressure cooker, then my mom drove me to the other side of the river to get the first sample at the yacht club. Like the first time, it was low tide but there'd been a lot of rain.

I waded into the LaHave with the Maxwell Pole, careful on the slippery rocks, wearing my rubber boots. I scooped up water and screwed on the sterilized lid.

Me doing parallel testing with Coastal Action in Bridgewater.

I was back home in less than an hour. Dr. Maxwell met us with the control and I prepared the testing cards.

Mom kept me company as I took the test cards down to the basement.

It was even harder this time to wait thirty-six hours. What would I do if the control had blue dots again or something else went wrong? The due date for my science fair project was in February. To have convincing results I needed to test the river more than once and over the longest period of time possible.

I woke up on November 29 and ran downstairs in my pyjamas.

I am determined to get accurate results this time.

Mom was in the kitchen getting her first cup of coffee ready.

"Put your coffee down! We have to get the cards! Come on, let's go!"

She left her cup on the counter, switched the light on to the basement and led the way. I walked one step behind her, down to the incubator. I opened the door and together we peered inside. There were the five cards.

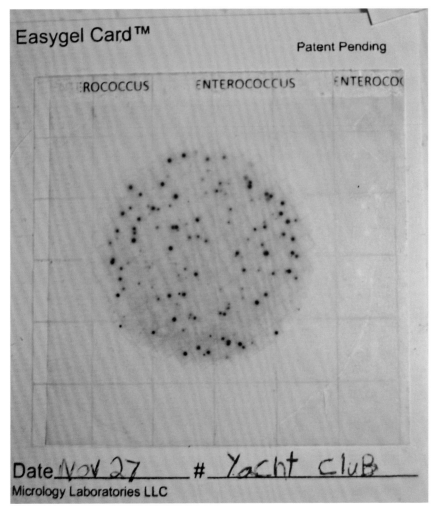

My brother was in that water! All those kids were in that water. No, no, no!

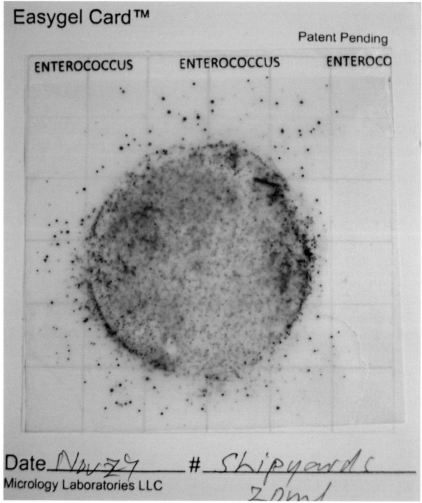

Can this be real? Is the water really **THAT** polluted!

One was completely clear. I breathed a sigh of relief and checked the label. Control. A clear control meant these results were scientifically reliable.

One of the cards was a blur of blue dots.

Mom and I stared from it to each other, horrified.

"Oh. My. God!"

I checked the location of the site. "Shipyards in Bridgewater." It was only a twenty millilitre sample. I had to multiply it by five to apply the Health Canada standards. There must have been thousands of dots. It was worse than I thought.

I took the cards upstairs to the kitchen table. Before I tallied the counts, there was someone who needed to see this. If I could convince my dad that my results were scientific, that the river *had* to be cleaned up now, I had a winning chance of convincing other adults it was time to fix things.

I ran upstairs into my parents' bedroom. Behind me, I heard Mom on the phone with Dr. Maxwell.

"Wake up, Dad! I took my test cards out of the incubator. You have to come and see."

Sleepy, Dad followed me to the kitchen table. Mom handed him a cup of tea to help him wake up. He stared at the five cards, took a big sip of tea, and stared again.

"What am I looking at?"

I showed him how Health Canada explained what the blue dots meant.

Alarmed, he put his cup down. His gaze shifted between the two worst cards. "This is terrible."

Suddenly he smiled at me. "You're really onto something. This is empirical evidence. I'm proud of you doing this project."

Did you know?

PRIMARY CONTACT: Recreational activity in which the whole body or the face and trunk are frequently wetted by spray, and where it is likely that some water will be swallowed. Inadvertent immersion, through being swept into the water by a wave or slipping, would also result in whole-body contact. Examples include swimming, surfing, waterskiing, whitewater canoeing/rafting/kayaking, windsurfing or subsurface diving.

SECONDARY CONTACT: Recreational activity in which only the limbs are regularly wetted and in which greater contact (including swallowing water) is unusual. Examples include rowing, sailing, canoe touring or fishing. (Health Canada, 2012)

I am so determined now to make this public. People need to know. I am on a mission.

Dr. Maxwell's car appeared in the driveway. Dad opened the door and Dr. Maxwell hurried into our house, wearing what looked like slippers but were in fact his favourite sandals.

Dr. Maxwell scanned each card visually. "Your numbers will be shockingly high. When people see them, let's hope they call their MLA."

While my parents and Dr. Maxwell talked politics, I sat down to tally the results. It took over an hour. In the end, I gave up counting the dots on the Shipyards Landing card.

Dr. Maxwell had gone by the time I posted my results on Facebook:

LaHave River Yacht Club: 145 enterococci/100ml
Upper LaHave: 110 enterococci/100ml
Dayspring: 310 enterococci/100ml
Shipyards Landing, Bridgewater: too many to count

I asked my followers to share these results. They did. There were 393 shares and the post reached almost 30,000 people within a few days!

Dr. Maxwell had advised me to do more tests using a different variable. My next date would be in December, but since temperature didn't affect the amount of bacteria I had to choose something other than a cold day. I chose precipitation levels. The first samples were taken after a lot of rain, so I picked an afternoon when there'd been none all week: December 10.

Dad came home early from his new job to drive me to the four sites. Here are the results I posted on Facebook twelve days later:

LaHave River Yacht Club: 89 enterococci/100ml
Upper LaHave: 160 enterococci/100ml
Dayspring: 800 enterococci/100ml
Shipyards Landing Bridgewater: 1005 enterococci/100ml

I am happy to report Bridgewater was countable this time, but really gross numbers still. Also, enterococci only comes from warm-blooded animals, so not fish poop. Fish are cold blooded.

PLEASE SHARE

Some people commented online that the bacterial contamination could be caused by duck poop, not human poop. Every time I waded in and out of the LaHave I saw gross stuff that only humans could have flushed down their toilets, directly through straight pipes and into the river.

The local newspaper asked me to respond to those comments. On January 6, 2016, they put my photo on the front page and quoted my response.

Giving my first interview in a radio station in Halifax.

I remembered the nasty things I'd seen. I didn't have to think hard about my answer. "The last time I looked, ducks don't use toilet paper."

Chapter 10
Let's Make a Video

To display my science fair project, I printed out colour charts of the test results and wrote up the background information about the LaHave River, straight pipes and *enterococcus*. I arranged it all on a big fold-out display board. I love colours and used bright markers — lots of hot pink — to highlight headings and important details.

On February 19, the school gym was packed with a hundred Grade 5 and 6 students, arranged in aisles with our science projects. Other classes came in to look and ask questions. So did judges from the community. They had to choose ten projects they found worthy of going on to the regional science fair in Bridgewater on March 31.

The announcement of the winners was made just before dismissal. My parents and William were there. So was Dr. Maxwell. The judges called out eight names. I clapped for each student named, prepared for disappointment. There were only two names left.

"Stella Bowles."

Did I hear my name? I stopped breathing for a few seconds. I stared at Mom, Dad, William and Dr. Maxwell. They were smiling at me. Clapping.

My project was going to the regional fair.

On the way home in the car, I said, "Was anyone else worried in there? I didn't think they were going to choose my project."

Mom said she was confident until the fifth name was read out.

CBC came to my house and did an interview with me for TV.
This was my first experience with TV, but not my last!

Dad felt much the same way. "I told myself, judges have personal taste. If this had been a music competition and your project was heavy metal and they liked folk, they wouldn't choose yours. What would you do about the LaHave River if your name hadn't been called?"

Outside the window the contaminated river flowed quietly to the ocean. As much as I liked competition, my goal went beyond winning a science fair. I wanted to keep people talking about straight pipes until no one used them.

"I'd keep testing the river. Can you take me out one more time this winter? I want to find out what's affecting the results. They're different each time."

Dad took me out the following week and here's what I posted online on February 28:

I tested the river again this week. Now I have 4 sets of results, so I made a graph.

Please note, when I put Bridgewater at 1100 enterococci/100ml, It is because it was uncountable! . . .

My findings suggest that even in colder temperatures, there is still a dangerous level of fecal bacteria in our river . . . Thanks for all your support. By the way . . . I am going to the regionals for the science fair on March 31.

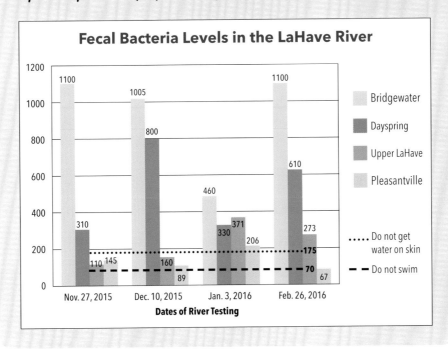

The CBC called, asking for another interview. On March 2, Paul Withers drove from Halifax to our house with a cameraman. The interview was aired the next night at six and another article was posted on their website.

Paul Withers introduced me as a twelve-year-old girl. I was too young to vote but I was forcing politicians to talk about saving a river.

They also interviewed the mayor of the Municipality of Lunenburg, Don Downe, because on March 8 the district

council was going to discuss applying for an infrastructure
grant to tackle the problem.

"This is an environmental disaster. This water is so bad.
Not only can you not swim in it, you can't boat in it. They
are saying now you should not even touch the water. It's that
contaminated," Downe told CBC News.

Over supper my parents explained that in order to get
this grant, three levels of government had to agree to
contribute an equal share of funding for a complicated
— and controversial — program. Replacing straight pipes
with septic systems would require legislative enforcement
by the province (responsible for the environment) so they'd
supply one-third. The federal government had to kick in
the next one-third because they had a big pot of taxpayers'
money for environmental problems across the country.
The municipality of Lunenburg, our local government,
would provide their third in the form of a loan which
homeowners had to pay back. Altogether the program of
removing straight pipes was expected to cost over $13
million.

I went with my dad and nanny to the municipal council meeting. It
was a very, very long meeting.

The municipality invited me to attend the meeting. Why not? I had to miss school (which was okay). That meeting was long and boring. I sat between Dad and my grandmother. I couldn't believe how long adults talked. On and on. To me, the solution was obvious.

I wasn't the only one fidgeting. Beside me, Nanny dug in her purse for her bag of mints. Each time she unwrapped one, *crinkle, crackle,* someone turned to stare. *Crunch, crunch,* someone glared.

After three hours I was starving. Nanny passed me a granola bar. *Crinkle, crackle, crunch.* More stares. I smiled at them.

Finally, they took a vote and decided they needed more information.

Here's what I posted on Facebook:

> Well, I went to this VERY long meeting and it wasn't a no vote and it wasn't a yes vote. I am staying positive. As a kid, it seems like a no brainer to vote yes.

Why was it so hard to decide to apply for funding? What more information did they need? I soon learned they needed to know if voters would support them.

That night at the supper table my parents explained why the government wanted to take time to talk to voters. They'd done nothing for way too long; I'd made it clear they had to take action. They wanted to educate the public about it. Some people had put in expensive systems already and resented that any rich people on the river who still had straight pipes would get taxpayers' money for two-thirds of the cost of a new septic system.

The mayor, Don Downe, called me "the living face of the issue." His office was totally supportive of a cleanup and called to discuss a smart idea they had.

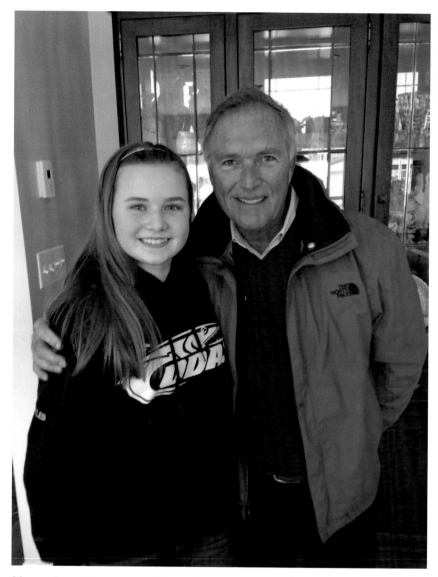

Mayor Don Downe came to my house to help with the river video.
He really wants a clean river, too.

   They wanted to make a short promotional video called "Our
Living Future — The LaHave River." They'd film me testing the
river and talking about my dream of swimming in the LaHave
one day. They'd also film me at the regional science fair on

I am so excited that I won the Science Fair. Dr. Maxwell was happy, too.

March 31. Then in April, they'd host four information meetings around Lunenburg County and show the film. Don Downe and other politicians would attend as many meetings as possible. Residents could ask questions and voice their concerns.

On March 31, I set up my project for the regional science fair in Bridgewater. The municipality made sure to invite politicians from all three levels of government. A film crew recorded me.

All the politicians said, "Let's put an end to straight pipes."

I won gold and the film crew followed us home.

Mom and I wore our boots and walked down to the river where I had to collect a sample of water while a drone flew overhead.

It was science in action and a cool way to end a very cool day. The video wasn't about me. The star of the show was the LaHave River. All of us cared about her. She was very sick. Yes, people wanted an end to straight pipes, but would they support a government program or fight it?

Mom put her arm around me as we walked up the slope, away from the river. The drone left the river, too, focused on us. We had to be the voice of the river.

I thought back to how I'd left a school because the rules were too strict and arbitrary. Rules had to be enforced. They also had to make sense to people.

Dad had dinner waiting for us. We'd invited Dr. Maxwell to join us. We sat at the table for a long time, the mood celebratory, talking about the many successes of the day.

"Using social media was smart," Dr. Maxwell said. "Despite all the advocacy I did, our group never got as far as you. The government never made a video about the river's future before. Three levels of government showed up today. Tonight, I have hope. Let's hope it wasn't just a photo-op with Stella to make them look as if they care. Let's hope they *do* something."

My brother had also been at the mayor's office for the long meeting. He asked a smart question, "One level had a chance two weeks ago. How long will it take three?"

Mom, Dad and Dr. Maxwell shared a look.

Every time I collect samples, I take time to appreciate this place I call home. My river is so beautiful. It deserves better.

"Could be months. No one knows," they said.
Everyone helped clear the table and clean up the kitchen.
I knew what I had to do. Keep up the pressure. People had to keep bugging the three levels of government to agree to a plan.

Chapter 11
Keeping Up the Pressure

Community meetings seemed like the perfect place to sell my Girl Guide cookies.

April 26 was the fourth, and last, public information meeting around Lunenburg County. This one was in Riverport. As with all the previous meetings, the community centre was packed.

The evening began with someone from the mayor's office showing the video, then answering questions. The previous meeting had been attended by one of our MLAs, Mark Furey. I'd brought Girl Guide cookies to sell at each meeting, so of course I'd asked him if he'd support us. He'd bought two cases and said, "I'll send these to Navy personnel deployed overseas." I'd brought another case and was disappointed he wasn't there again tonight.

Like the other nights, people involved in the issue stood at tables; I stood at one with my project. Across the room several people from Coastal Action fielded good questions at their table.

The mayor stood at a table beside me. I overheard an elderly woman say, "I have a straight pipe I don't like to have, but I live on a fixed income. I'm scared I'll lose my home. What will I do when you ask me to pay back the loan? I won't be able to."

62

This is the community meeting team. We were all there to answer questions. Some people were not happy about the river plan. Sometimes fair isn't always equal. I am told that in school a lot, but adults often seem to forget that.

The mayor nodded. "I understand your fear. You'll probably qualify for a grant to pay it back. And there will be people to help you make the application."

A man nudged forward. "What about the homeowners who do have money? Do they deserve to get the benefit of government funding? I did the responsible thing and put a septic system in five years ago. Why should someone who can afford it get a break? That's not fair."

The mayor responded, "I understand it may feel unfair but we have to move forward and focus on our goal." He pointed at the title of the video up on the screen.

"This is our chance to end straight pipes. This program will make a cleaner river for everyone's benefit. It's what everyone deserves."

"Aren't livestock a possible source of contamination? What will you do about runoff from pasture land?" asked another person.

"You're talking about upriver, above Bridgewater. Coastal Action has tested there and yes, it seems to be another source of the bacteria. If you go to their table, they'll tell you more about it," responded the mayor.

"Isn't there a farmer who keeps his manure pile right beside the river?"

"Yes, and all we can do right now is suggest he move it."

At every meeting, we'd heard the same comments. People agreed with wanting a clean river but not how to do it fairly. When people came to my table they were supportive of my science project, even my sign. Except one homeowner we'd nicknamed the TM. Dad came up with the nickname after we overheard someone call the man a troublemaker. He'd attended every meeting, flushed with emotion, and always challenged my results. "How do you know those blue dots are poo dots?" His complaints at the other tables were even louder and more critical.

Tonight, Dad saw him first. "Oh oh. Everybody shield Stella. Get ready. The TM is coming our way."

My parents and William stood in front of me as a shield. The TM made a comment we'd heard other nights.

"I swam in the river as a kid and never got sick. Look at your results. The highest numbers are in town. That's the real problem."

Before I could answer, he fired off his next comment.

"You're dreaming if you think ending straight pipes will

end pollution. There are worse sources of contamination. Why don't you test the duck pond outflow and the town sewers after a storm? What about the sewage treatment facility? Make the government fix those problems."

Mom shot me a warning glance. *Do not engage.* The TM moved to the next table to speak with the Environmental Services Manager, Tim Hiltz.

William turned to talk to me. "Straight pipes are disgusting, Stella. It has to get fixed."

I nodded. "I've figured out how to change my project for Grade 7."

The TM's conversation with Tim Hiltz was too loud to ignore. "Your facility is the main source of pollution. Stella Bowles should study the sewage treatment facility!"

Tim Hiltz responded quietly, "You're right. Yes, we are a source . . ." and he continued to explain what they were doing.

The man listened to Tim Hiltz intently, calmer, his anger gone. He was still concerned, but then to my surprise, I overheard him say these meetings had helped him understand that the government was trying to fix the problem.

The event organizers flicked the light switch. Time to go home.

The public left, including the TM. We packed up and walked out with Tim Hiltz.

"That man probably has an illegal straight pipe he doesn't want to fix," Dad said.

Tim Hiltz nodded. "He's not alone. But I respect his tenacity and that he came to every meeting and is thinking hard about the big picture. He's coming around. I think these meetings were useful."

"Wait until they announce the program and start to enforce it," Dad said. "Three levels of government are going to hear a lot of complaining."

"I hope they come to an agreement soon," Tim Hiltz said. "We owe our kids a clean planet."

I liked his positive attitude and decided to float my idea past him.

"I have to change my project a bit for next year's science fair. If I test the outflow of the duck pond and the one from your facility to prove there are other sources of contamination, will the government stall or speed up agreeing to a program?"

"Neither," he said. "They already know the main sources of pollution and that it's time to enforce a cleanup. If you get them to end straight pipes, you actually make it easier for me to get a grant to improve the sewage treatment facility. We each play a part in this. If we're on a path to clean up the river, the more people that talk about *all* the sewage issues, the better."

When I talked over my new hypothesis with Dr. Maxwell, this is what I came up with: There are more sources of fecal contamination in the LaHave River than just illegal straight pipes from homes discharging untreated sewage. I started work on it right away by contacting Coastal Action. They said they'd be testing the river at the new sites I was interested in and would let me know when in case I wanted to come along.

That spring a series of good things happened: David Suzuki gave me a Blue Dot shout-out; I was nominated for Starfish Canada's Top 25 Under 25 Young Environmentalist Award (I didn't win); and I was introduced to the provincial legislature (and got a standing ovation).

I was also invited to give presentations at schools, museums and to a Native Council meeting. I wasn't nervous. It was exciting to speak to people who wanted the same change I

I presented my project to the local Mi'kmaq Council. Their support is important to me.

The Mi'kmaq Council gave me a dream catcher with a teepee in its centre, representing the home we love.

did. The Mi'kmaq Council gave me a dream catcher with a teepee in its centre, representing the home we love.

Coastal Action took me out with their crew to sample water from sites above and below Bridgewater. I did my own testing and posted my results.

Before I did, Dr. Maxwell reminded me that testing for enterococci in fresh water is a bit different, so I only posted salt water results from Bridgewater and downriver.

I couldn't forget the TM's question: How did I know for sure those blue dots were really enterococci? He had a good point: I needed to be sure.

I went to Province House in Halifax. What a beautiful and busy spot!

Dr. Easy's lab at Acadia University was very cool!

Mom contacted a scientist at Acadia University, Dr. Russell Easy, who agreed to help me answer that nagging question. My brother was equally curious and came along the day we drove to Wolfville. So did Dr. Maxwell.

Here's what I posted on Facebook as well as a photo of those dots under the microscope:

After school today I went with my mom, brother and Dr. David Maxwell to Acadia University to do a bit of science. I was curious to see what those blue dots looked like under a microscope. With the help of Dr. Russell Easy, I took 4 different colonies from the enterococci testing card and stained them with a Gram stain. They were all Gram positive cocci in individual and short chains.

This testing is consistent with enterococci, therefore this shows the blue dots on my testing cards are actually poop. It is amazing to see what the bacteria looks like.

Thank you Dr. Russell Easy for offering to show me how to do this and for the use of your lab. Science is so cool.

William really enjoyed the science, too.

Chapter 12
My Big Mouth

I invited friends to join me at a council meeting and they came! This was a great show of support for the big announcement. I was so nervous the councillors would vote no.

The big municipal vote was planned for Tuesday, June 14, 2016.

"I'm going," I told my parents.

"Me, too," William said.

We invited friends to take the morning off school with us to show them kids cared about the river. My dad called it a "sit-in."

The meeting was long and boring, but this time I felt a stronger connection between my goal (no more straight pipes) and their goal (no more straight pipes).

CTV and CBC covered the event on the evening news. Here's what I posted on Facebook:

> This morning was the big vote in the Municipal Office. I am super happy to report that all councillors except for Councillor Ernst voted YES! Thank you everyone for your support. This is a great first step to cleaning up the LaHave River. Thanks to all my kid friends for coming to council as well. We are the future and need to have a voice! I think we were heard. I'm so happy right now.

What I didn't post was that a hostile reporter happened to call us, trying to scoop a good story by discrediting my home-grown testing methods. I was late getting home from school and fortunately Dr. Maxwell was there to explain — in serious scientific detail — we'd thought of all the things that could go wrong, and we'd done parallel testing.

Not long after that, we got another phone call from the mayor's office. They invited me to attend a press conference on July 7.

What a great way to begin summer — being part of that day.

In front of reporters and cameras, the municipality and the provincial government signed an agreement regarding their compliance program to eliminate ALL straight pipes into the LaHave River.

It was empowering, as a kid, to be part of a team with these players: the mayor, the councillors, MLAs, the Minister of the Environment and our MP.

Even though the federal government hadn't agreed to

I am right in the middle of a whole bunch of politicians.
I can't believe they are hearing my message. I am so proud.

anything yet, our local MP, Bernadette Jordan, was there and keen to speak with me. She promised her support and said there'd be plenty of meetings and memos in Parliament about this cleanup. It was just a matter of time.

Over the next week I helped my brother clean and paint his sailboat. We wanted to enjoy our river even if it had to be on top of the water. Once the sailboat was moored offshore Dad and William decided the safest way to get to it was in the paddleboat (instead of wading out as they used to). It was

I showed a group of kids from the Annapolis Valley how I test my river.

It was fun to share my science and meet new friends. This day gave me a new idea!

almost funny to watch — and hear — them go out. William jumped easily from one deck to the other but Dad fell in and the big splash covered my horrified brother with water. They paddled back to shore and both ran up to the house to take long, soapy showers.

I met Prime Minister Trudeau. This was a great moment for me.

The high point of my summer was meeting with a group of kids (and their parents) from the Annapolis Valley. They'd contacted me, eager to learn how to test their local river for fecal contamination. I took them to the sites I'd chosen for my Grade 7 project and we scooped up samples of LaHave water with the Maxwell Pole.

Back at home, Dr. Maxwell helped me teach them the procedure. What a great summer day, all of us interested in using citizen science. It got me wondering: Could I teach *more* kids to test the contamination of their local river or harbour? The cost of the kits and an incubator would be the biggest hurdle. I was lucky because not only did Dr. Maxwell lend me an incubator, he persuaded the LaHave River Credit Union and Coastal Action to generously sponsor the purchase of all my testing supplies. I'd need funding to start a mentorship program. It would have to wait until after I'd done all I could to heal my river.

One year into taking on the LaHave River cleanup, I'd learned something about politics and about myself. I had a voice. I liked public speaking, being in front of a camera and meeting important politicians like Justin Trudeau, our Prime Minister, which I got to do in August. How cool was that!

But in September, I faced an event that skyrocketed me out of my comfort zone.

I won the Evergreen TD Future City Builder Award. I was invited to fly to Toronto for a gala dinner and give a speech to a lot of adults — strangers in Ontario. Why did a group of strangers in Canada's largest city care about what I was doing in my small corner of rural Nova Scotia?

Fortunately, my dad came with me. I told him how nervous I was and he made me laugh.

"Think of 'The Emperor's New Clothes,'" Dad said. "Imagine the audience has no clothes on. It will help you relax and feel less nervous about being up there in front of everyone."

Thankfully, I didn't need to use this trick. The organizers introduced me by talking about the importance of science fairs and making the world a better place. We were on the same team, too.

"What you did inspires all of us," they said. "Young and old. In Canada and around the world. Your science fair project went beyond the classroom."

They asked if I had any news on the federal agreement. I replied that we expected them to sign soon. The cleanup was supposed to start on March 31, 2017.

Flying out of Toronto, I looked down at the huge expanse of tall buildings and roads spreading from the edge of Lake Ontario to the horizon. Millions of people. Constant noise and traffic. I noticed, too, a river winding its way through the city to the lake and remembered how nervous I'd felt arriving here two days earlier. Although I couldn't wait to get home I'd been warmly welcomed at the gala. I'd felt connected to the people I'd met. They cared about making the world clean and beautiful the same way I did. Tim Hiltz was right: We are all working together to clean up the environment. We are one big team.

Me with my dad at the Evergreen Brickworks Gala in Toronto where I received the TD Future City Builder's Award.

Mom picked us up at the airport and drove us home. The federal government was still saying nothing, but getting off the highway Mom shared an amazing piece of good news.

"Someone from the South Shore is contributing one million dollars toward building the new septic systems!"

My mouth fell open. I was stunned into silence as I thought about what an incredibly generous act it was. Someone *really* cared about our world and was an important team player behind the scenes.

"Who is it?"

"It's an anonymous donor."

"Why don't they want anyone to know who they are?"

Dad said, "We'd have to ask the person. I'm guessing they don't consider their name to be important the way celebrities do. They want the focus to be on the action: donating to the community."

"Whoever it is," Mom said, "they have good business sense. The donation was made to the municipality to help fund their third of the cost of each new septic system. That's the part homeowners will get as a loan, remember? The provincial and federal government parts will be outright gifts. When homeowners pay back the loan the municipality will be able to use that pot of money to fund other programs."

Dad whistled. "Beautiful. The gift that keeps on giving."

I was floating on a cloud of optimism all the way home. After I unpacked and we were sitting around the supper table, Mom brought me back down to earth, "Even if they break ground and install the first septic system next spring, they're predicting the program will take six years to complete."

"Six years?" William's eyes nearly teared up. "That's way too long. Are you kidding me? I'll be in high school before I can swim in the river."

It makes me happy that many people are working together to clean up the environment.

Dad said, "There are over 600 homes still using straight pipes. Think about it. That's a lot of planning, trucks, material, workers, digging. It will take time."

We had to accept it, but it was hard to be patient as we waited for confirmation that the federal government was on board with the project. Every night, William and I asked if there'd been any news, phone calls or messages.

A week passed with no news. Hockey games, Girl Guides, swimming — I was busy — but those weeks crawled by, turning into months. Only silence from the federal government. No one knew why it was taking so long.

I did my regular tests along the river, the same four sites as the previous year, as well as the new ones around the

This is the duck pond outflow location.

outflows of the duck pond and the sewage treatment plant. Every month I posted the horrible results on Facebook. All were bad, but after it rained, the results at the two outflow sites were the worst. Dramatically worse.

March 31, 2017 came and went. Silence from the federal government.

I made it to the regional science fair again with my Grade 7 project. The event was held in Bridgewater on April 6. I was disappointed with the government but happy to win a place on the Nova Scotia team going to the national competition in Regina, Saskatchewan in May.

But I had work to do on my science fair project; the judges in Bridgewater criticized how I'd presented my results.

"This isn't about activism," they said. "Stick to the science and redo your display."

The lead teacher in the science fair committee recommended specific changes I should make. "Take out all personal photos," she said. "No photos or quotes from the media. No mention of Facebook or meeting the Prime Minister. Stick to your hypothesis: Are there other sources of fecal bacteria contamination in the LaHave River? You can reference the test results from Coastal Action about farm runoff as a source of contamination, but use the words 'results seem to indicate . . .'"

Mom and I spent long hours redoing the display. I took out the photo of me with Justin Trudeau. I said nothing about my real-world goal: ending straight pipes into our river. It wasn't hard because I was passionate about the science and the topic.

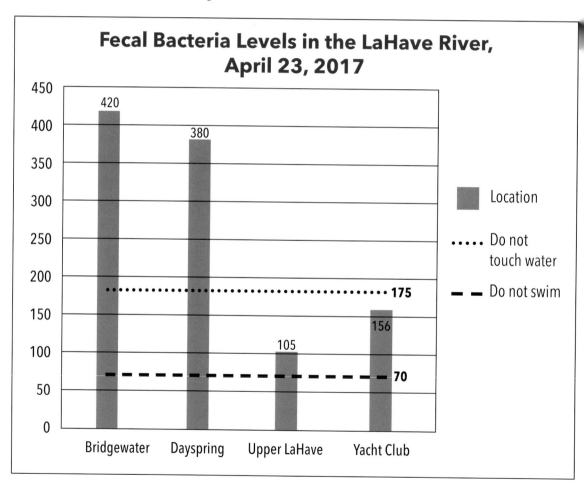

I learned to make a chart on my computer because a chart shows results in a way that's quick and easy to understand.

The federal government's silence — *that* was the hard part.

The science fair judges didn't need to know about my activism, but my neighbours, other kids, the media and the government did. I was not keeping quiet. Here's what I posted on April 23, 2017:

It has been a while since I posted results. I am still hopeful the project to rid the LaHave River of straight pipes will go ahead, but at this point, the federal government has not announced their part of the funding. I must admit, I am nervous and hope people don't just decide to stop fighting for a cleaner river. I'm not going to stop. Straight pipes are illegal and adults need to fix this. It isn't right. It is just so, so wrong!

**PLEASE SHARE THIS POST TO REMIND PEOPLE THAT OUR RIVER IS EXTREMELY SICK AND NEEDS HELP!

I'm going to keep fighting for a healthier LaHave River.

Chapter 13
It's Really Happening

I had a wonderful week in Regina at the Canada-Wide Science Fair. There were over 500 students competing. That alone was inspiring. The other three students from Lunenburg County were older than me and had fantastic projects: one arose from the drought we'd experienced during the summer of 2016 and used cool science to prove that polymers helped retain 37.5 per cent more water in a dug well; one studied the effect of exercise and stress on gene expression; and the third project studied Lyme disease which was on an alarming rise in Nova Scotia.

On the third day before winners were announced our teacher–chaperones told us to expect lots of judges to come by and ask questions. I noticed fifteen, maybe twenty, judges walk past me to other displays. When my group compared experiences at the end of the day my heart sank. *All* the judges had talked to the other students on our team.

I shared my experience. "Only three stopped at my project this morning and none this afternoon."

"Only three?" said one of the teachers, frowning. "That might not be a good sign."

I texted Mom immediately. A sad text.

Mom tried to be encouraging. "Maybe they know all about your project already. It's had so much media attention. Did they ask you anything unusual?"

I thought back over their questions. One of my answers seemed to win a nod of approval.

"They asked if I had any new projects. I told them I

84

planned to train other kids how to test for enterococci and that I was applying for funding to buy their supplies for them."

I was surprised and really pleased when they announced the winning projects. I brought home a Silver Medal and two of the other students from Lunenburg County brought home Bronze!

I hoped my award might nudge an announcement from the federal government but two more weeks of silence went by. On June 3, this is what I posted to Facebook:

I won a silver medal at the Canada-Wide Science Fair in Regina. It was an amazing week in Saskatchewan!

I really enjoyed the Canada-Wide Science fair and I did very well there. My happiest moment will be when illegal straight pipes are dealt with, especially in my river.

A lot of people worked hard on planning the project to clean up the LaHave River and I am very worried now that the Federal money won't come and once again, people will stop caring about cleaning up straight pipes.

I can win all the awards in the world, but if change doesn't happen, I really haven't won a thing. :(

CBC was following my posts on Facebook; a week later they wrote another article about the issue, headlining that we were still waiting for federal money.

Mom read the article out loud at the supper table over a pizza dinner. I half listened as William and Dad made comments. I couldn't take my eyes off the photo under the headlines: our big sign beside the river. Twenty-one months of testing, posting, speaking and attending meetings since I'd put that sign up. Twenty-one months of waiting.

"Last June," Mom read, "municipal council voted to apply for seventeen million dollars from Infrastructure Canada in order to remove the 600 or so straight pipes that dump 600,000 litres of grey water and raw sewage per day into the river . . ."

Oh my god. That was the worst thing. Twenty-one months multiplied by 600,000 litres of grey water every day . . . it was too disgusting to do the math.

"Our Liberal MP is in the dark," said Mom. "She's in touch with the minister's office and they say it's working its way through the system, but we expected the announcement back in March."

"Doesn't look good," Dad said. "What does Dr. Maxwell call it . . . ?"

"Bafflegab," William said, turning to me. "Bafflegab sucks. We gotta do something different."

I stared out the window, then smiled at William.

"It has to be something to make people phone their MLAs and MP. Something to cut through the bafflegab. I know just the thing."

They liked my idea.

As soon as my new sign was ready we went out to the river as a family and put it up.

600+ HOMES FLUSH THEIR TOILETS DIRECTLY INTO THIS RIVER

No action meant I had to spark the conversation again. I think this new sign will work beautifully!

Here's what I posted on June 18:

> I put up a new sign. Sadly, this is a LaHave River fact.
> Please **LIKE** and **SHARE** this photo.
> I expect adults to soon address this **SERIOUS** environmental problem.

This post reached over 120,000 people in one day.

A week later my dad and I went to Montreal where I received the Wade Luzny Youth Conservation Award from the Canadian Wildlife Federation. I got a standing ovation.

Four days later, the announcement that everyone was waiting for happened.

Here's what I posted on June 29:

THE LAHAVE RIVER WILL BE STRAIGHT PIPE FREE IN SIX
YEARS!:)

Today, my MP Bernadette Jordan announced the Federal portion of the
river clean up plan. This makes me so happy. Thank you to all three levels
of government for coming together to make this happen for the future of
our LaHave River.

Please LIKE & SHARE this great news.

Oh . . . and I took the opportunity to sell my strawberry jam to the
politicians . ;)

The river cleanup plan received the federal money AND I sold more of my jam. That's what I call a win-win!

Epilogue

I took the sign down because things are happening now. I think it did a great job educating people.

Stella was asked to take down her sign in September. She agreed because the government promised that their program would start soon. It did.

The program officially began on November 30, 2017,

breaking ground to prepare a site for the first septic system installation.

Here is what Stella posted on her Facebook page:

Well, this is exciting! Our river will be cleaner with each straight pipe removed.

Winter weather interrupted the work of the LaHave River Straight Pipe Replacement Program. Even so, by the end of 2018 they hope to have 100 new systems installed.

True to her word, Stella has successfully expanded her focus from healing one waterway to healing many around the province of Nova Scotia. With the help of donations, she's teamed up with Coastal Action to train other kids on how to test for fecal contamination. If you're interested you can contact Stella through her Facebook page (LaHave River: Stella's Science Project) or Coastal Action in Lunenburg at (902) 634-9977.

There was more good news in March 2018. Just as Tim Hiltz, the Environmental Services Manager had hoped, the wastewater treatment plant in Bridgewater was awarded $750,000 from the Government of Canada Clean Water and Wastewater Fund to upgrade and improve their system.

All across Canada, all around the world, we need to take better care of the earth and each other. Stella noticed a problem in her backyard and shouted the truth — for nearly two years.

She didn't tell adults how to fix it. She just said, "Fix it!"

She continues to study the pollution in the LaHave River but from a new angle: foraminifera. Look it up. It's cool.

Activism starts at home. Gandhi is often quoted as saying: Be the change you wish to see in the world. Find mentors and

In the fall of 2017 sample sites were dug to test the soil and design the systems. Stella was invited to a groundbreaking ceremony in April 2018. It marked the end of straight pipes and a new beginning!

other people who want the same change you do and *lean in together.* Create a tipping point.

It's empowering to make your corner of the earth safe and beautiful.

Imagine if we all did.

— Anne Laurel Carter

Acknowledgements

A lot of people have helped me and they really want to make the LaHave River better for future generations. Without their support, the river project would not have been possible.

Thanks to Shanna Fredericks, Emma Kinley and Brooke Nodding from Coastal Action Foundation. They were very supportive of my project and even took me out on fieldwork to do parallel water testing. I look forward to learning more from you all in the future. You are doing great things for our local environment.

Thank you to our previous and current mayors of the Municipality of the District of Lunenburg, Don Downe and Carolyn Bolivar-Getson as well as Alex Dumaresq. Also, Steve Warburton who made the LaHave River video. It was so much fun to help create, especially with the drone.

Thank you to the provincial government MLAs, Mark Furey, Suzanne Lohnes Croft and previous Nova Scotia Environment Minister, Margaret Miller. Your dedication to ensuring the LaHave River cleanup will continue into the future has been awesome. I truly hope we can now get the province to enforce the elimination of illegal straight pipes whenever a house is sold in this province. It is the next logical step to make.

Thank you to my MP, Bernadette Jordan, who was very supportive of cleaning up the LaHave River from the start of my project. Also, thank you for introducing me to Elizabeth May and Catherine McKenna and showing me around Parliament Hill. It was inspiring to meet so many women in politics and for all of them to encourage me to do more.

There was a small group of people who formed the LaHave River Straight Pipe Committee, and I joined them. Thanks to

Wayne Mulock, Yvonne and Laurie Rafuse and Mary Lane who came to monthly meetings and taught me so much about what was already done to help our river.

Thank you, Dr. Russell Easy for letting me use your lab at Acadia University and showing me how to Gram stain. It was a fun day! My younger brother really enjoyed it, too.

Thank you, Tim Hiltz for giving me a tour of the Bridgewater Wastewater Treatment Plant and discussing with me the future plans to continue separating rainwater pipes from sewer pipes. You taught me that there are many people committed to making the systems better. I know you are working hard for positive change and applying for grants to improve the overall infrastructure.

Thank you to Jane Berrigan and Chad Frittenberg for being the teacher-chaperones for the Canada-Wide Science Fair in Regina in 2017. I am glad I had the opportunity to spend a week with you and learn to love science even more, even though you took me to a cadaver museum.

Thanks to many neighbours and friends who supported my project and giant sign. I know it wasn't a sign anyone wanted to see in our neighbourhood, but I think it did draw attention to a problem below the surface of the river that we couldn't see.

A big thanks to all the people who supported me on my Facebook page. Your likes and comments really inspired me to keep going.

Dr. David Maxwell was my mentor and biggest supporter. He was always there when I had questions or concerns, ready to help me in any way this project turned. He will always hold a special place in my heart. Thank you, Dr. Maxwell.

Most importantly, I would like to thank my mom, Andrea Conrad, dad, Lender Bowles, brother, William, and nanny,

Carolyn Conrad, for walking this journey by my side and always encouraging me to ask questions and advocate for what is right. We really did this as a team.

— Stella Bowles

I love my home.

Index